The Power of the Next Small Step

What's the Best that Could Happen?

Rayya Ghul

The Power of the Next Small Step
What is the Best that Could Happen?

By Rayya Ghul

This book may be purchased for general reading or promotional use. This is not a medical journal or a manual. The information in this book is for general reading and general understanding only. Author does not hold any responsibility of any consequences related of misunderstanding of reading. It is always advised to seek proper medical attention for any need.

No part of this book may be used or reproduced in any manner without written permission expect in the case of brief quotations in critical articles and reviews.

Table of Contents

About this book

This isn't a book about how to get rich, find the love of your life, make a business work, get your children to listen to you, lose weight or make millions. It is not step-by-step, expert advice on how to achieve specific things you might want. It is something far more useful, as I will explain.

I could tell you what's worked for me to get my children to listen to me, but my children aren't your children. You are not me. You probably don't live where I live, and maybe you don't even live in the same country. In other words, expert advice only goes as far as we are willing or able to put it into action. Sometimes it simply does not 'fit' with our particular situation.

Instead, this book is about how to live a sane and successful life using a remarkably simple approach called 'Solution Focus'.

Solution Focus was originally coined as a name for a form of brief therapy developed by Steve de Shazer and Insoo Kim Berg, family therapists in Milwaukee, USA. The approach then found its way into other areas of work such as life coaching and organisational development. It is now widely used within health and social care, business and education worldwide. But it has been a well-kept secret known only to the professionals in these sectors and those with whom they have worked.

I began using Solution Focus in the early 1990s when I was working as an occupational therapist in a mental health team in England. Since then I have trained numerous professionals to work using a Solution Focused approach.

Friends and acquaintances often ask me if there is a book they can read to find out more about Solution Focus. This book aims to bridge that gap.

Everyone is able to use a Solution Focused approach. It is easy to learn and with a little practice becomes a natural alternative to 'problem-solving', which, as you will see, isn't always the way to the best solution.

Dedication

To my beautiful and talented daughters, Nashira Daisy and Miranda Rose. You have always been my greatest teachers and inspire me daily. You are my most precious gifts.

Introduction

We cannot solve our problems with the same thinking we used when we created them. –Albert Einstein

This book will introduce you to a simple way of engaging with life, which enables you to find your own solutions to problems and your own route to move forward towards your personal goals using the skills, knowledge, and resources you already have.

This simple approach to life is called 'Solution Focus' and at heart is built on one simple principle:

Find what works and do more of it!

If it's that simple why have I written a whole book about it? Well, 'simple' doesn't always mean easy. In some ways the fact that it is simple makes it harder to put into practice. However, the good news is that with a little practice, you can learn to use a Solution Focus to improve your life forever!

The Solution Focused approach to living comes from a form of therapy called Solution Focused Brief Therapy, which is used to help individuals, couples and families overcome mental and emotional distress, change unhealthy behaviours and improve relationships. It is a very effective therapy, but unlike traditional psychotherapy it works very rapidly, typically between 3-8 sessions.

This is because solution focused brief therapy differs in one important way from all other forms of psychotherapy. In Solution Focused Therapy *you do not need to know anything about the problem in order to come up with solutions*.

Pause for a moment and let that sink in.

How do you normally try to solve your problems?

If you go for help or advice to a friend, family member or professional, what usually happens? I reckon you will spend some time, maybe a considerable time, describing your problem or difficulty. You may try to work out why things have gone wrong or what is wrong with you or other people. You may go back through your past, looking for what went wrong. You may look for who or what to blame. You may spend time complaining about how hard things are, how unfair life isand how nothing you do changes anything.

You are given advice which, while well-meaning, is often inappropriate, something you've already tried or something you would never do!

Sometimes, you will come up with solutions and some of them may work. However, a lot of the time you end up feeling worse because you feel hopeless or you find yourself complaining about the same thing over and over again and feeling increasingly stuck. Even if you end up feeling better for having talked about it, nothing is different.

Imagine having those same conversations but instead of spending time describing the problem, you discuss how you would like things to be in the future.

Instead of going over the past looking for what went wrong, you spend time looking at what is going right and which you could build on. Rather than examining your flaws and mistakes, you identify your strengths and resources.

Instead of getting advice, you come up with realistic, creative and sustainable solutions which fit with your lifestyle and values.

Instead of complaining about things out of your control, such as other people or the economy, you spend time identifying the most useful action you can take *right now* which might make a difference. And when you take those first steps, instead of saying: 'Well, what's the worst that can happen?' You say 'What's the best that can happen?'

There is an old saying, 'if all you have is a hammer, every problem looks like a nail'. Similarly, if you are used to always using a problem-solving approach, life looks like it is full of problems to be solved. Situations become problems. People become problems. Life's challenges become problems, and so on.

As we shall see, trying to understand the problem and what 'went wrong' rarely helps unless the problem has an easy and logical solution. Of course if it did, then you would do it - problem solved! What usually happens is that you feel overwhelmed, confused, inadequate or defeated and it's hard to think of what else to do to move forwards.

When you shift to a Solution Focus your world will slowly change for the better. You start to see situations differently. People appear different, and you start to see challenges as opportunities. Most importantly, when you start to explore a situation using a solution focus, you

4

have more confidence that your efforts will make a difference. You can start to take small steps towards a better outcome because you are able to see possibilities previously hidden by problem thinking.

That is when you create the power of the next small step.

However, this is not about 'positive thinking'. Although you will certainly become more positive about yourself, your life and others. It is not about simply visualising a better future and hoping it will come true. Solution Focus is a powerful technology for change which has been tested and proven to work for thousands of people.

The Solution Focused approach has been adapted for use in life coaching, organisational development and management change, education, youth work and social work. It has been shown to work when problem-solving approaches fail. People from very different traditions, languages and cultures use it all over the world.

Practice makes perfect

I will give you the basic tools so you can put Solution Focus to work straight away. Like any new skill it requires practice. Throughout the book you will find exercises to do.(You might want to go and get a notebook and pen before starting to read further.)The exercises are the key to start making the changes you want to see and move towards a better future. Unless you do the work in the exercises, it is doubtful that you will get the full benefit of Solution Focus. This is because your problem-solving habits are so strong and some of the processes initially may seem illogical or counter-intuitive. As I will explain further on, *problem-solving* is seductive and will engage your mind when what you really need is to be using that energy on working out how to move forward.

Solution Focus is built on a series of questions which orient you towards what you want, what you have right now and how to use your strengths and resources to move towards your preferred future. These questions are different to the ones we would use for problem-solving. I will explain the difference in the next chapter, *Myth-Busting*, as well as showing how problem-solving may even have prevented you from moving forwards.

EXERCISE: You are reading this book for some reason. Before you go on, stop and think:

What is your best hope for what you could get out of it?

What is it you would like to change or create?

Unless you go through the process of answering Solution Focused questions, this book will remain little more than words on a page. You need a different kind of thinking. Solution Focused questions help you develop it.

When you take the time to do the exercises and take the small actions as a result, it will become a new way of life where making decisions, overcoming difficult situations and having the confidence in your ability to do this effectively are second nature.

Chapter One

Myth-Busting

When you look at yourself through the problem-solving lens,

it's easy to imagine that you have lots of faults.

The Problem with Problems

Problems are like whirlpools, once you start talking about them they can suck you down into a spiral of blame, shame, hopelessness and despair.

We know our problems very well because we go over them again and again in our heads or in discussions with friends and family, picking them apart, trying to find causes, deficits or blocks which might give us clues to solutions and create change. If you think about a sticky problem you have shared, you probably expect that the person listening will ask questions such as 'When did it start?' 'What went wrong?' or 'How do you feel about it?'

This seems quite logical because we have been brought up from an early age to approach the world with a problem-solving mindset. There is nothing wrong with this! Problem-solving is extremely effective in a huge number of human endeavours. If my car breaks down I want my mechanic to identify what went wrong and fix it. If I become ill, I want my doctor to find the cause and cure it.

Here are the three basic approaches to problem-solving:

1. **Find something that isn't working and fix it.**

2. **Find something which is missing and replace it.**

3. **Find something which is causing difficulties and remove it.**

This is a brilliant, logical approach and works most of the time. For example in medicine:

- **If a bone is broken, it needs to be set.**

- **If the body is not producing insulin, a person needs to inject themselves with it after meals.**

- **If the patient has an inflamed appendix, it needs to be removed.**

However, there are often limits to problem-solving. When you have tried variations of these three approaches you tend to run out of options. This is why people with 'untreatable' conditions such as chronic pain and disability are frustrated by their encounters with doctors and other health professionals. They are frequently told they have to 'live with it' or worse. In the case of chronic pain, they can be told their experience is 'psychological' so they feel doubted.

Most of the difficulties and distress we feel in life are not, strictly, 'problems'. If they were, we could solve them fairly easily with the right tools and skills.

In Solution Focused living we do not spend time examining problems in detail.This is not because we are not interested in our own and other people's difficulties, it is because there is little to be gained from doing so, and it will waste time.

Not only can it do that, but it often makesyou feel bad to dwell on your problems which, if apparently 'unsolvable' can result in an increased sense of powerlessness and hopelessness. At best, a conversation may be comforting and make you feel cared for, but actually changes nothing.

Most of the difficulties and distress we feel in life are not, strictly, 'problems'.

If they were, we could solve them fairly easily with the right tools and skills.

The Big Myth – What is normal?

Underlying the problem-solving approach is a very powerful myth. This myth is a relatively recent human invention and I believe it is a dangerous and damaging myth: There is such a thing as 'normal'.

If you learn only one thing from this book, this would be it.

There is no such thing as 'normal'!

Even machines have quirks; car engines built from the same components develop different problems. 'Normal' is a picture in your mind of what the perfectly functioning version of a bicycle or a heart would be like, a handy mental tool. It is useful because if you are looking for something to fix, take away or add, it provides you with a template to work from. It is the problem, solved.

Solution Focus also makes use of the idea of the problem solved, but in a different way to the problem-solving approach. In Solution Focus, the problem solved is unique to the person. Whereas in problem-solving it is a pre-determined ideal. If you are mending a watch, this is useful, but it you apply it to a person, it is problematic.

I don't know about you but I have never met anyone just like me although I do see similarities with others. No one I know is exactly like another. Even if we were all born identical, the experiences and environments we grow up in would make us different. So why do we think that there is such as thing as a 'normal' person?

I suspect the idea of 'normal' became popular in the 20th century when modern medicine and psychology seemed to promise the possibility of curing and healing everyone. Put that together with mass media and advertising and you can see that the messages about what is 'normal' and not have been used to encourage conformity and social stability, as well as encouraging us to aspire to ideals of behaviour, beauty and lifestyle.

Every good idea has unintended consequences, and many people feel they have fallen short of these ideals. This has led to widespread unhappiness and a feeling that we are not good enough, beautiful enough, smart enough or successful enough.

The next chapters examine a few of the common myths about change. They will help you to understand why Solution Focused living focuses on what we want our future to be like and what we can do right now towards making that happen, rather than dwelling on the problem and past difficulties.

No one is exactly like another.

There is no such thing as NORMAL!

MYTH No.1: You have to change before anything else can change

Myth One is connected to the idea that there is a 'normal' or 'ideal' person that you should be. Experts in psychoanalysis and psychotherapy have used this notion to treat trauma and mental and emotional distress with many positive results. However, on the downside, they have also given the general public a message that we are damaged by our negative experiences and that damage can only be corrected by engaging with a professional or through some kind of psychological practice.

It is not surprising to think you need to become a better person, more sorted or good looking to move forward to achieve what you want. This myth is subtle because it appears to be so logical.

But what does it actually mean? What do we have to change?

For the answers, we usually look to psychological descriptions. We have to decide that we need to improve our 'self esteem' or develop 'confidence' or 'will-power', as though these were as tangible as the muscles in our arms and legs that we develop down at the gym.

What we are doing is engaging in a *problem-solving* approach to ourselves. We are looking for something which has gone wrong, something to fix, or search for the missing part. When you look at yourself through this lens it's easy to imagine that you have lots of faults. Pretty soon you are convinced of all your flaws and weaknesses!

So let's go back to the myth – in which you need to change yourself before anything else can change. If you are using a problem-solving approach then you may spend considerable time and money on self-improvement or self development activities. There is no shortage of people or businesses willing to help you become a better person to help you achieve your dreams.

There are two drawbacks to this approach. First, it takes time. Second, in order to take this approach you have to find fault with yourself. In fact these two drawbacks work together. The more you try to 'mend' or 'correct' your faults or 'heal' your hurt, the more you find. This takes even more time! Years can pass before you begin the life you really want to live or think you deserve, given you are so 'flawed'!

What's the alternative? When you take a solution focused approach to living, you start out with a different view of yourself. Sure, you're not perfect (who is?) but at the same time, you have some decent skills, strengths, qualities, talents and resources, which have enabled you to survive and thrive so far. So at the very least, you are adequate for the task, and probably well equipped.

You are also designed to change and adapt. It is built into your nature. Notice that as soon as something around you changes, you change in response to it. You respond all the time to your environment. A lot of the time you are completely unaware of these changes. In Solution Focus we make this natural process of change work for us. By engaging more consciously with change we set a better direction, and take small steps towards what we really want so we change naturally. There is no need for years of critical self-reflection or therapy. If you need help with changing aspects of yourself, there are plenty of resources around.[1]However, when living from a Solution Focused perspective we only use these resources when we need them. And we know the purpose that this investment will play in our lives.

---

[1]My personal favourites are Rhonda Britten's 'Fearless Living' and Natalie Liu's 'Baggage Reclaim'.

19

Solution Focused living starts you moving towards what you want in your life and change happens as a result. You change, people around you change and your life changes.

EXERCISE: List 10 qualities or talents you possess that have helped you make positive change in your life, however small.

EXERCISE: Look at yourself in a mirror. Instead of finding faults look for your best features. Smile and enjoy them!

MYTH No.2: Something big has to change before anything else can

Often you do not start to make changes or you get stalled because you think that you need something big in your life to be different. Perhaps you need a lot of money or to be living somewhere different. Maybe you dream of the day when you'll win the lottery or your ideal partner will show up. Then things can really change! This is the source of the *'if only's* and *'yes, but's* in your life.

Your ambitions may be grand or simple; either way being able to feel some degree of control of your destiny seems important. When you perceive a large obstacle or enormous lack which seems insurmountable or something is unachievable, you can limit your possibilities and therefore your satisfaction with your current situation.

When you are living with a Problem Focus, obstacles or lack are viewed as something you have to problem-solve. f there is no clear and immediate solution then you tend to give up. Obviously there are many people who take on a challenge and do anything in their power to overcome adversity but they tend to be the exception, driven by a passion most of us do not possess.

There are also people who are able to accept their situation with complete equanimity, happy with what they have. They are lucky, I envy them. However, in my experience most people fit somewhere between these two poles, living with greater or lesser degrees of dissatisfaction, wishing something were different, if only.

When you shift to a Solution Focus, obstacles and lacks are transformed into something much more interesting. They can tell you about what you really want and value in your life. Once this becomes clear, the means to attain what you want may be closer than you think and not even what you originally thought at all!

EXERCISE: What are your *'if only's*? Is it more money, a different house, a new job, or partner?

Pick one and write down 10 answers to the following question:

'If I had that, what difference would it make?'

Now, what does that tell you about what is really important in your life?

MYTH No.3: We can know all the facts about a problem

In order to solve our problems effectively using a problem-solving approach we need to know a lot about the component parts. This is because we are looking for *something to fix* to make everything work smoothly again. When our problem is very complex and involves people, this becomes pretty much impossible! However, this doesn't stop us from trying to work out all the problems – often keeping us awake all night.

We think that if we try hard enough we can know all the facts, and if we don't then we make them up in order to feel more in control of the situation. For example, you might say "My daughter is difficult" if you are having trouble creating a harmonious household. You may have identified her as the 'faulty' part of the family. You may try to correct her faults ("Clean up your bedroom") and if this doesn't work, she turns into an obstacle to your happiness. You say: "If only my daughter was ..." and when other people offer suggestions you say, "Yes, but she is so difficult!"

When you feel you should be able to know all the facts you become susceptible to other people's 'facts' especially if they appear to be authoritative or offer the possibility for a solution. In desperation, you may take your daughter to an expert and you could be told she has 'oppositional defiance disorder' which might require treatment, even medication. Like a faulty part, your family member needs to be 'corrected'. This rarely goes well.

The rest of the family either feel relieved of responsibility and the daughter ends up feeling isolated and defective, or worse, the family then look to themselves for further 'facts' - which usually translates into blame."If only I hadn't spoiled her/punished her/sent her to a childminder."You make up even more facts in the attempt know everything about the problem's history. Ultimately you end up with a fractured family, each with their own set of 'facts' about the problem because they feel obliged to produce them to explain the mess you are all in. Does this sound familiar to you?

Solution Focus will not magically change people, nor will it make you see the world through rose-tinted glasses. However, it will offer you different possibilities for dealing with the complexities of life and human relationships. Solution Focus does not require you to know everything in order to create meaningful and lasting changes in difficult situations. It does not help you come up with perfect solutions every time.

However, it does produce solutions that respect the diversity and complexity of human life and allow everyone to be treated with dignity and consideration.

When I worked in mental health I saw many people who felt despair at their apparent inadequacies, lack and damage. Applying a Solution Focus helped them slowly to regain a sense of their unique strengths and resources and see those in others. Sometimes this was dramatic and sometimes it was a slow process. Undoing all those 'facts' about the problem is often hard because they form part of the story of our lives and our identities. To give them up or consider alternatives can feel very threatening. It is also true that most people are trying to do their best and be happy. What's more, if the way to that becomes clear (and seems possible) then it is easier to move in that direction and leave the old habits behind.

Feeling the need to know all the facts often leads us into examining the past for causes for our present problems. This is another problem-solving activity. This implies that the world is a series of causes and effects, a complex machine. While it is true that certain types of traumatic events or upbringing do have lasting consequences, examining the past generally sheds a little light on events rather than transforming them.

You may gain understanding about *why* you feel and behave the way you do You may be able to let go of some of those feelings and behaviours and, therefore, take advantage of positive opportunities. However, what more often happens is while you may understand why you are the way you are, you still don't manage to change substantially. You may know *why* you pick emotionally unavailable partners, for example, but you still don't know how to form a healthy relationship with confidence.

Your insight can become a comfortable narrative to explain your failures. At worst it can become disempowering if you have extensively mined your past for 'facts' and still haven't produced meaningful change.

While self-knowledge and awareness are undoubtedly useful they are often still rooted in a problem perspective and cannot become tools for change. For that to happen, a shift in perspective is required. Without that you could revert to your belief that in order for change to happen you have to change, so you do *more* self-examination, 'deeper' analysis of the facts and so you go round and round in the problem-solving cycle making yourself or others either problems or causes of problems.

EXERCISE: Have you got an excuse that you keep using for why you can't do something?

Imagine that your past is like a computer hard drive which has been wiped clean so the excuse has been completely erased.

What is possible for you now?

List at least 10 actions you could take.

MYTH No.4: Knowing all the facts about a problem will help you solve it

Complex problems generally involve aspects that are outside of your control. Perhaps your life is difficult because you have lost your job. This is a 'fact' you know. Perhaps you lost your job because there was an economic crisis. This is another fact. Just because you know these facts, there is nothing you can fix - knowing that you lost your job because there was an economic crisis doesn't mean you can then mend the economy to make it better and then get a job!

Sadly, in these circumstances people often turn on themselves with a critical gaze, and try to work out what they did wrong to end up being the person who lost their job. Asking "Why did this happen to me?" is a good way of generating self-blame and criticism. We can always find some reason to beat ourselves up."I should have been more assertive.""I shouldn't have been so demanding.""I'm not as good as ..." and the even more ridiculous, "I should have known ..."

Again - problem solving may not help because it disempowers you, or worse, it makes impossible demands on you. When you adopt the problem-solving approach, you are limited by the problem. The problem acts like a filter on where you focus. It's always a solution to that particular problem.

On the other hand, if you liberate yourself from the problem and start by considering your *best possible future*, all of a sudden your focus is immediately on hope and possibility. You can become creative because you have the energy and the space to explore, and you are not wasting time on trying answer "Why?"

Some years ago I kept finding myself frustrated by a colleague at work who I perceived was blocking my career progression. I kept trying to find ways to resolve this without success. One day someone asked me "What would your ideal retirement look like?"As I described this, I began to realise that rather than try to deal with my colleague, it would be much more useful to begin to take small steps towards making my ideal retirement come true. I had imagined myself living by the sea, having helpful conversations with people and being creative. I took a jewellery-making class and started to focus more on aspects of my work that fitted in with this vision. In the process, the difficulty with the colleague faded and my life started to change.

The power of Solution Focus is that it encourages you to look at what you can do right now. It focuses immediately on *possibility* not problems.

EXERCISE: Think of a situation where you feel stuck. Now imagine yourself in a future where things are at their best.

What would be happening?

What would you be doing?

What small step could you take right now to make that possible?

If you liberate yourself

from the problem

and start by considering

your best possible future,

all of a sudden

your focus

is immediately

on hope and possibility.

MYTH No. 5: In order to find a great solution you have to spend lots of time talking about the problem.

If you have read through and understood the previous four myths and done the exercises, I hope you now see that you don't need to waste any time on the problem and can go straight to generating solutions.

If not, go and do those exercises NOW!

Here is the amazing insight the founders of Solution Focused therapy worked out and which makes it so different to other approaches.

You don't need to know anything about the problem to find great solutions!

You really don't have to waste time analysing the problem and asking 'why' you are in that situation when you are living with a Solution Focus. Focusing on problems is a difficult habit to break! But once you get this, your life will be transformed, with no more feeling bad, blaming or shaming or time-wasting on 'problems' required.

However big or small your challenges or difficulties, by focusing on the best possible future you will free your mind to generate multiple potential solutions. You will focus your attention on what works instead of getting bogged down by problems. Your vision of the future you really want will pull you forwards. And the next steps you need to take will become clear.

When my daughter was small she would run into the room and would make some demand or complaint in a jumble of words and emotion which were hard to understand and respond to. I found it exhausting. One day, I managed to remember to be Solution Focused and said to her: "I think you are trying to tell me something very important but I can't understand it because of the way you are saying it. Just pop out the door and think of a better way of saying it and then come back."I was amazed when she came back and stood up straight in front of me and then with perfect composure she said "Mummy please can my friend stay for a sleep-over. I promise we will be good."Just the suggestion that there could be a better outcome helped her generate a different behaviour.

> **EXERCISE:** Think of a situation you would like to change, however big or small.
>
> Ask yourself *"What would I like to be happening instead?"*

ONCE YOU SEE THROUGH THE MYTHS YOU REALISE:

1. There is no such thing as 'normal'.

2. YOU don't have to change before other things can change.

3. Change is not dependent on something BIG happening first.

4. We can never know all the facts about a problem. So don't probe.

5. Even if you know the facts about a problem it isn't always helpful.

6. In fact, you don't need to know anything about the problem in order to find great solutions.

Chapter Two

Becoming Solution Focused

The power of Solution Focus
is that it encourages you
to look at
what you can do right now.

It focuses on
possibility
not problems.

Getting on the Solution Focused track

It sounds obvious to say that when you focus on solutions you are more likely to find them. Most of the time you think that the way to find solutions is to analyse or unpick the problem; to determine how it started, what is holding it in place and what part of the problem needs to be addressed first. This is what we call *problem-solving* and while it works well with machines, and simple mechanical systems, it fares less well when applied to people and complex systems.

This doesn't stop us trying, of course! I think of problems as being like whirlpools. We hang about the edges, dabbling with what might be going on and then, whoosh! We are suddenly sucked in by the power of problem-solving and revolve round and round the problem without ever breaking free.

When you focus on the problem it becomes stronger, more 'in focus'. Just like when you focus binoculars on a tree you start to see it in greater detail. You become more familiar with it. When you focus on the history of the problem you see a logical progression which is hard to break. There is inevitability about how things will progress. If it's being going on for long, it becomes harder and harder to imagine anything different.

Fortunately the same applies to solutions. When you focus on what works, what has worked in the past and what you want from the future, a completely different picture comes into focus. You see the beautiful bird in the tree, and then you can see a few more. What you thought were leaves are greenfinches!

So, how do we start to develop a Solution Focus?

Creating the vision of your preferred future

The first and best place to start is let yourself dream about how you would like your life to be. We call this the *'future perfect'*: the future beyond our immediate problems. If your life is very difficult this can feel very remote and hard to imagine. It might even make you feel afraid to contemplate in case it makes you feel even worse or it feels 'unrealistic'. All of us have a comfort zone and feel uncomfortable when we step out of it.

Sadly for many people their comfort zone is anything but comfortable – it's often low grade misery. It can involve staying in an unhappy marriage, drinking too much, using addictive substances, having self-limiting or self-punishing thoughts or even physical self-harm. Often, staying with what you are familiar with is far easier than making changes to improve your situation.

If you can imagine a better future in great detail (with the problem solved), it acts as a catalyst for change because it allows you to enter another 'possible' reality, which you can explore and become comfortable with before taking steps to create it.

Using Solution Focus you can create a vision of the preferred future which leads to effective solution-building now. As you will see, this process can light the way out of even the most sticky life situations.

In my work with people with mental and emotional distress I ask people to imagine a 'miracle' has happened or that they have a magic wand which allows them to reconnect with forgotten dreams and with glimmers of hope. This touch of 'magic' works!

I remember a man in his 50s, called Frank, who suffered many episodes of psychosis throughout his life. During psychosis your brain produces hallucinations and loses its ability to make logical connections in the world. The medications used to treat psychosis are very strong and cause other serious health problems. Frank had never been able to work, had no friends and so led a very limited life. He spent most of his time in his one bedroom apartment smoking and watching television.

When asked what his life could be like if a miracle happened Frank's answer was very surprising. He said, "I would go and visit my brother in America. I haven't seen him for 30 years." No one in the mental health team even knew about this brother. The social worker went through the Solution Focused process with him, exploring this possibility in detail. Then, over the next few weeks, she helped him to take all the small steps he identified to achieve this goal: contacting his brother, arranging the dates, getting a passport, booking the flights and so on. Every day Frank gained more confidence. He began to wash regularly, dress well and eat better food and by the time he had been to America and back he was transformed.

Frank is living proof that you don't have to change first to make change happen!

Think about you and your life at its best. What is going to make it as meaningful and fulfilling as possible? This will help you determine the most effective path forward. Recent research has suggested that pursuing what is meaningful and valued by you is more likely to create a satisfying life than pursuing happiness So maybe happiness is a by product of a meaningful life.

> **EXERCISE:** Imagine a miracle happened and your life was the best you can possibly imagine.
>
> *What would you be doing?*
>
> *What difference would that make?*

Searching for 'exceptions'

The next stage of the Solution Focused approach is to look for 'exceptions'. These are the signs that your future is already starting to happen or they could be the parts of your life where things are going well already. Often you miss these when distracted by problems.

If you have clearly visualised what you want in great detail it gets a lot easier to notice these positive signs. For example, if you want to have a better relationship with your partner, when you are able to imagine what this will look like, you can begin to notice the times when this happens, even a little bit, and build on that. If you want financial stability you notice that when you budget, you are less likely to have difficulty paying your bills. If you want a more organised living space, you can see that you somehow manage to keep your bedroom tidy even if other parts of your home are messy. If you want to feel happier more often, you realise that when you walk through the park each day on the way back from work, it makes the evening more pleasant.

Also we tend to clump our experiences together and give them a universal quality. We say, "Oh I had such a bad day today" because the overall flavour of the day was heavy and unpleasant. However, if we deliberately look for something that went well, we can generally find it. The day was not ALL bad! Maybe the shop assistant smiled at you, you got a seat on the bus, your child was distracted long enough to have a conversation with a friend.

Positive psychology suggests that looking for things to be grateful about at the end of each day improves your wellbeing and looking for exceptions is similarly beneficial. Being grateful for the exceptions we find creates a powerful fuel for change.

Angela's Story

The power of focusing on exceptions was really brought home to me by a very special client with whom I worked. Angela had struggled all her life with very low self-esteem and as a teen she had developed anorexia. She eventually managed to start to recover and was able to train as a nurse and later as a midwife where she was particularly effective at working with parents of stillborn babies. Angela was a deeply spiritual person, a committed Christian who truly wanted to help ease pain and suffering in the world.

Unfortunately Angela was still battling with her negative feelings about herself. In her 30s she began to self-harm, sometimes seriously. She tried to keep it a secret but eventually it became known to her employer, and due to the sensitive nature of her work she was unable continue her work as a midwife. With her life's work dashed she found it hard to find any good reason to continue living apart from her fierce faith and when I met her she was lurching from one self-harm or suicide attempt to another.

At our first meeting I asked Angela the usual Solution Focused questions: "What would you notice different if a miracle happened?""What is happening now which is a sign that the miracle is already starting?"And what might her next small step might be? Angela was able to describe her future perfect in some detail but was unable to identify *any* signs in the present.

Before I left I asked her to spend the week noticing even the tiniest sign. We worked together for three years, an unusually long time, but sometimes people work at a slow pace and need more support. Angela gradually improved her life, and some years after I stopped working with her she came to a conference with me to do a joint presentation where we interviewed each other in front of an audience.

I asked Angela to tell me what she thought about our first meeting. This is what she said:

"When you first came you asked me some really odd questions and I did like talking about a miracle. But to be honest I couldn't see how any of it would be helpful. At that time my whole world was black, total darkness that was all-enveloping and all-pervasive. I remember you saying that I should try to notice any tiny exception - just notice it and then try to remember to tell me about it the next time we met. I really couldn't see the point but then three days later it happened. I noticed something different, tiny, insignificant, and it was like the first star appearing in the night sky. Gradually I saw more and more and it was the first time I experienced hope in many years."

If you go to a Solution Focused coach or therapist they will ask you a series of questions. These questions are specially designed to get your brain focused away from seeing problems and problem-solving and towards generating solutions and solution-building. In the next chapter I will give you these questions for you to work through by yourself or with a friend.

Are you ready to create positive change?

Chapter Three

Solution Focused Change

Solution Focus
uses your imagination
to explore
possibilities
so you can identify
action that can really
make a difference.

Tools for Change

In this section I will share the main questions that form the Solution Focused process:

How to identify your *preferred future* **or 'future perfect'?**

How to mine for *'exceptions'*?

How to identify your *strengths and resources*?

How to generate *small steps* **towards your preferred future?**

There is also a section on *'Coping Well'*. Sometimes things are so bad it feels like you are simply living from day to day and a better future feels very far away. Solution Focus can also help you stay positive while in your current difficulties and gently move you towards improving your situation.

I recommend you should use a special notebook or journal to work with this section. Write down the answers for future reference.

Alternatively, you may choose to work with a friend and ask them to ask you the questions. There is something powerful about hearing your own answers out loud. Record your answers on a mobile phone or digital recorder so you can play them back later.

Whatever way you choose, it is important to give yourself plenty of time to free your mind. Solution Focus uses your imagination to explore possibilities so you can identify action that can really make a difference.

Your Preferred Future

Generating a 'preferred future' or a 'future perfect' is the first stage of Solution Focused change. Be specific. You are aiming to build a rich description of how your life will be. The greater the detail, the more effective this part of the process usually is. You will find out what you really want and what motivates you. Some of this might surprise you!

The key to getting the most out of this exercise is to allow yourself to dream, to imagine different possibilities, to explore what you could do and be without the constraints of the past or present. It's YOUR unique future. START here:

PREFERRED FUTURE EXERCISE:

Choose *one* of these 4 questions to answer, and use the *expanding questions* in the next box to create the rich description

1. What if a miracle happened and all the problems holding you back disappeared? How would your life be?

2. On a scale of 1 to 10, where 10 is the best your life could be, what would 10 look like?

3. Imagine your life is like a computer and you can press a button and reboot it, deleting all the bad things which happened in the past. How would it be different?

4. What's the best that can happen? *(This question is useful if you are considering a particular life situation in the near future, such as going for an interview, or working out how to resolve a conflict*

EXPANDING QUESTIONS:

List at least 10 answers to each of the following questions to create a richer description of your preferred future:

1. What would be happening?

2. What would you be doing?

3. What would other people be doing? E.g. your best friend, a parent, a work colleague

4. What would people be saying about you?

5. How would you be feeling?

6. What would your environment be like?

7. What would you be looking forward to?

8. How would you know things were going well?

9. How will you be maintaining this positive preferred future?

By now you should have a really good description of the future. To make this even more meaningful and motivating, there is a very special question you can ask.

> ## 10. What difference would that make?

If you have written out answers to the list of questions, now go back and ask this question of *each* answer you gave. Then ask it again of the answer you just gave!

For example,

"What would be happening?"

"I'd be rich."

"What difference would that make?"

"I'd be able to buy a big house"

The effect of asking this question is that it helps move you from the general to the personal. A lot of people want to be rich. It doesn't tell us much about that person though. The second answer is a little more personal. But again many people would like to own a big home. However, if we keep asking this question the answers get more and more personal and specific.

Here is an example of a real conversation I had with someone continuing from those two:

"What difference would that make?"

> "I'd have plenty of space for my grandchildren to come and play."

"What difference would that make?"

> "I'd feel like I was a good mother and grandmother."

Very quickly we have moved into what really matters to this person, let's call her Patricia. Incredibly I then found out that Patricia didn't yet have any grandchildren! I was much moved. What a lovely person! This was a very deep and meaningful dream of hers and it had been uncovered in only four questions.

Try this exercise for yourself and see what your first answers really signify. You might even be amazed to discover that what you really want is a lot easier to attain than you thought. Being a good mother and grandmother is something Patricia could start doing *right now* without needing lots of money.

From now on you can just ask *"What difference would that make?"*Each time you will generate an idea for an even better future. It is really helpful to ask that question when next you are facing a decision or choice.

When you answer these and other questions in this book, try to avoid negative answers, such as "I wouldn't be shouting at my children."If you write something negative down, ask yourself *"What would I be doing instead?"*

Once you have a really rich description of the future which is so detailed you can almost feel it, touch it or even smell it, you are ready to move on to the next section. Don't worry if your future seems far away or unrealistic, *'Mining for Exceptions'* will help connect your preferred future to your life right now in a very real way.

Mining for Exceptions

Now that you have created a clear picture of your preferred future, however big or small, you need to return and connect with where you are right now and who you are at your best.

This is because without some connection to your present life you cannot move forward effectively. Much as we might like to think that the force of our will or the powers of our imagination are enough to 'create' our life, you will still have to start from where you are right now.

However, in Solution Focus, the way you look at 'right now' is different, because you are not going to focus on what is wrong. Instead you are going to look for all the *exceptions* to the problem or difficult situation as well as for evidence that small parts of your preferred future are already happening. If you really work hard in this section, you will see your current situation quite differently.

When you work with a Solution Focused therapist or coach they will gently but persistently ask questions to try to identify these special times. Exceptions not only make you feel better about your situation, they will also give you vital clues as to how to build solutions and remind you of skills, knowledge and strategy you can utilise on the way.

I like to talk about 'mining for exceptions' because it can take some effort to shift your focus from the habit of lumping together and categorising your experiences as somewhere between catastrophic and absolutely fabulous. You have to chip away, slowly uncovering the smallest sign that things are going well. It is all too easy to overlook them especially if you are focused on your problems or negative situations.

There are four main ways of mining for exceptions.

1. **Look for times your 'preferred future' is happening now.**

2. **Identify a difficult situation and then look for times the problem isn't happening.**

3. **Look for them in your past.**

4. **Look for actions that work in one situation which could be applied to another.**

I will now go through these four options with you. This will work best if you have already done the exercises in the previous section *'Your Preferred Future'*.

The more information

you have

about what works,

the easier life gets.

1. **When are times when parts (or all) of the preferred future is happening?**

If you have done all the exercises on generating your preferred future then you can review your answers. Take a look at your life and see if you can identify times when parts of this are happening right now or in the recent past. If NOT – please go back and answer the preferred future questions.

When you spent time on identifying the difference achieving your preferred future will make, finding this type of exception can be very fruitful.

Try using the scale of 0-10 to generate what 10 would look like, then look at the scale and ask yourself *"Where am I now?"*(The 0-10 scale is No.2 of the Preferred Future exercises in the previous section.)

It doesn't matter what number you choose - it's not an exact science, just what seems right to you. If it's anywhere between 2 and 10 then you can ask, *"How do I know?"* and *"What am I doing right now which is helping me?"* As always, try to write as long a list as possible. Keep asking yourself, *"What else?"* until you really can't think of even the most insignificant sign.

If your answer is 0 or 1, then you may need to get a friend to help you ask these questions or even consider getting some professional support from a Solution Focused therapist or coach. Go to the *'Coping When Life is Hard'* section of this chapter for more ideas.

2. When are the times when the problem isn't happening?

Identifying exceptions requires a shift of focus towards seeing even the tiniest sign that things are going well or working. When you are feeling low or stuck, it is very hard to see positive signs. However, making the effort to notice even the smallest sign that things are going well, starts to break down the pervasive sense of things going wrong or badly.

Instead of seeing a situation or a person in black and white terms, try to identify or notice the times that are different, however small.

In Angela's story we saw how looking for exceptions to the total darkness she was experiencing led her to spotting tiny signs of her preferred future which allowed her to slowly rebuild her life. Most of us are lucky enough not to be gripped by such a powerful negative state. But we can still find ourselves feeling stuck or overwhelmed by a situation.

This is a useful exercise if you find yourself using words like 'always' and 'never' or if you are using absolutes like 'terrible', dreadful', 'bad' or 'awful'.

You can either take a piece of paper, try to write down as many exceptions as possible, or you can simply make the effort to notice exceptions as you go through a day.

When you notice an exception, stop and ask yourself *"How did I do that?"*The answer(s) to that question may be a clue to what works and something worth doing more of. This exercise is really useful if you are trying to create a lifestyle habit such as healthy eating or exercising more.

As you know, we resist change, but there are times when it feels effortless. These are the times worth investigating. A little caution though, if your answer is a feeling, such as "I felt motivated", that doesn't tell you much as feelings come and go and are not easily controlled.

If you wait to 'feel motivated' you may never go to the gym again. However, you can ask yourself *"What was I doing around and during the time I felt motivated?"*Then the action(s) you identify can be repeated.

To build on the exceptions you find, try to identify what is different about the times when things are going well. Ask yourself:

"What am I doing?"

"What are other people doing?"

"Where am I?"

"What time of day is it?"

Remember, the secret to Solution Focused living is to find what works and do more of it. The more information you have about what works, the easier life gets.

3. In times past, what things were different (better)?

Looking for exceptions in your past is closely related to the search for exceptions in other parts of your life. It is remarkable how difficult situations can blind us to the fact that things haven't always been this way. It is common during hard times to negate every past success. Despite numerous good things happening, the natural inclination is to focus on one hurtful criticism or challenge. Don't beat yourself up!

I find the past to be one of the richest sources of exceptions when working with people experiencing mental and emotional distress. There are many different ways of mining the past for evidence of what works. You can look at the strategies you used to deal with similar situations. Alternatively, you can simply think about what was different at a time in your life when things were going well. Then you can identify the conditions that enabled success.

Some Solution Focused therapists may ask about a 'sparkling moment' in your past when things were going particularly well. Others may ask you to recount a difficult event but help you to reframe what happened, so you can see your own strategies for developing resilience and survival.

EXERCISE: Take some time to reflect on your own past

1. What successes do you see?

2. What skills have you forgotten about?

3. What did you do previously in a similar situation which worked?

4. How did you respond well to difficulties in the past?

5. What are you most proud of achieving?

6. What would your friends say you did well?

7. Which part of the past do you want to bring with you into the future?

An expanding question for exceptions is to ask yourself:

How did I do that?

4. **What actions, which worked in one situation, could be applied in another?**

We often compartmentalise life, e.g. between work and home or a leisure activity. Because these are different contexts we sometimes do not notice that the skills we use in one context are precisely the ones we need to apply in another.

It is easy to take for granted that what you do is normal and unremarkable simply because you can do it. I really encourage you to make an extensive list of your skills and then take a look at a situation you would like to change or where you feel stuck. Could any of those skills be useful?

A powerful question you can ask yourself is *"what am I like at my best?"* I am sure you can answer that one!

EXERCISE: Think about all the roles you have.

What are the skills you use to fulfill those roles?

How do you do that?

It is easy to

take for granted

that what we do

is normal

and unremarkable

simply because

we can do it.

Your Strengths and Resources

What are your strengths and resources?

This is a surprisingly hard question for most people to answer. We are generally uncomfortable with saying nice things about ourselves in case we are seen as boasting or big-headed. More than that, we seem more comfortable putting ourselves down or comparing ourselves with others and coming up short. When we are given a compliment we may brush it aside or attribute it to the person's kindness rather than our qualities.

Looking for your strengths and resources is a type of exception-finding. Instead of looking for times when things are going well or when your problems bother you less, look for exceptions to the negative stories you tell yourself about who you are.

Here is a powerful question you can use to help identify your strengths. You can write the answers on a piece of paper or you can get a good friend to ask you them.

Sometimes it helps to be able to say these things out loud.

> **EXERCISE:** Think about a hobby or social activity you engage in outside of work. Now ask,
>
> *"How do I do that?"*

This is a deceptively simple question and to get the most out of it, try and describe the answers in great detail. You probably take what you do for granted and see it as normal and unremarkable. But once you finish the list, take a look at it and ask yourself what strengths and qualities you can identify.

For example:

Not everyone can read a book from beginning to end. *What does it take?*

Not everyone can organise a children's party. *What does it take?*

Not everyone has the discipline to exercise every day. *How do you do that?*

If you are getting a friend to ask you these questions, he or she might like to listen out for strengths and qualities and feed these back to you. What did they pick up about you?

I hope you are pleasantly surprised by what you find out. One of my missions in life is to help people see how wonderful they are. Just being a human being, surviving and thriving in this complex world means that you must have skills, strengths and qualities. Many people simply don't realise this and hold on to negative views of themselves or put themselves down. Much of the work I did as a therapist was to break down the old, unhelpful perceptions people had built up about themselves.

Remember: Nobody's perfect!

One of the most negative side effects of the problem-solving approach is that we have become focused on finding faults and deficits to correct in ourselves. There is an illusion that there is a perfect human which we must aspire to become. This is an ideal person who has a perfect body, never gets moody, is able to do everything and knows exactly what they need do. The problem-solving approach requires some sort of 'ideal' against which to judge ourselves. It is about calling something 'normal' and then being concerned about what falls outside that range.

This is all fine when we are talking about machines or if you are a doctor testing someone's blood pressure. In those cases, knowing what is ideal or normal is actually useful. Unfortunately parents and teachers often think they are being helpful when they tell children what is wrong with them, even with the best of intentions. This advice can be deeply damaging as children tend to believe what adults tell them, and often adults hold on to these negative ideas.

I encourage you to let go of the need to correct yourself. *You are who you are today and tomorrow you will be different.* If you want to change in a particular direction, you can. This book will help you do that. But please do not feel you have to dislike any part of yourself at this moment in time.

What are your values and principles?

As well as strengths you also have values and principles by which you live. These help to guide your choices and actions. You can find out what these are by using another simple question.

I'm smiling as I write this, because when I teach Solution Focus I always use this as an activity. I get one person to complain to the other for three minutes. The person listening isn't allowed to say anything, just listens hard for another person's positive qualities. At first, people think this is impossible. So I suggest they think about what kind of person would complain about the type of thing they are complaining about. For example, someone who complains about things not being fair is someone who cares about justice. Someone who complains about rudeness is a person who values good manners.

Try this out with a friend. The only rule is that the person listening MUST NOT say anything! It's harder than you think to stay quiet. You'll find yourself wanting to agree, disagree or give advice, because this is how we normally try to solve other people's problems. What that actually does is feed the problem. See what happens when you stay silent and then just give positive feedback about all the qualities you noticed.

If you are doing this exercise on your own, it may be a bit harder. I suggest putting on a three minute alarm and just start writing, uncensored, for the whole time. Then stop and take a look at what you've written and see if you can spot your values, principles and qualities.

What are your resources and support systems?

Finally, you should identify your resources, the support systems you have and things which help you through life. You can start to list these or simply make a list of everything in your life for which you are grateful.

Whenever I feel down, if I start saying what I am grateful for out loud, I soon start feeling happier.

Let go of the need

to correct yourself.

You are

who you are today

and tomorrow

you will be different.

Small Steps to Your Future

Now that you have identified your preferred future and have worked out where you stand in relation to it right now, you can begin to move towards it. This is when the magic happens!

I chose to call this book 'The Power of the Next Small Step' because I think all the preceding work to identify your preferred future and exceptions,strengths and resources are the foundation for the real engine of change; taking action. Having said that, without that preparatory work to identify exactly where you are heading and real clarity about where you are right now in relation to that destination, your actions would not have the power they do.

In Solution Focused living we move forwards by taking small steps, which we hope will make a difference and bring us closer to the life we would really like to live. You may be used to using goal-setting to achieve change. But this is not the same as the 'small steps' approach.

There is nothing wrong with setting goals, especially if we require milestones to reach an ultimate aim. Goals are good if you are training for a marathon or if you are planning your workload. However, when you are trying to make changes in your life, and particularly if this involves people or other uncertain factors, goals can be problematic.

First, success and failure are attached to the achievement (or not) of a goal. Obviously success is great but failure is unpleasant and de-motivating to most people.

Second, setting goals is less *helpful* than identifying small steps. This is because goals imply some ability to tell the future, predicting exactly how our actions will bring about a desired outcome! In this sense, goals are actually fantasies - even the ones that appear most 'realistic'! How sad then that if we don't achieve a goal or it doesn't turn out the way we wanted, we feel a failure.

Small steps, on the other hand, are like little experiments. Something we can do and then see if it makes a difference. Sure, they require commitment but not too much investment. We don't have to go too far down a path before realising it isn't taking us in the right direction. On the other hand, if a small step brings benefits, we know to do more of it.

So how do we decide what to try out?

Well, when you did the exercise on 'mining for exceptions', you may have identified some strategies or actions which worked in the past and which you might not have noticed previously or thought significant. You may choose to do more of these. *Remember the central idea of solution focus is to find what works and do more of it!* So if you have found something that worked previously, it is worth trying again.

You may simply think of something you could try out. If you created a preferred future using a scale from 0 to 10, then look at the point on the scale that you identified as where you are NOW. Hopefully, you spent some time looking at how you know you are at that number.

Now you can think, *"What might be a useful small step to take me a bit up the scale?"*and *"What difference might that make?"*

Remember, this is a *speculative* step. You don't really know if it will help. But if it does work, then it gives you useful information and helps you determine the next step.

Why is this important? For example, if you want to create a more organised workspace, then it is fairly easy to take a small step, such as buying a storage box.

However, if your situation is more complex, like creating a better relationship with your work colleague, then things are not so much in your control. You could try something like making the effort to smile at them first thing in the morning. Or offer to buy them a coffee. Something will change but not necessarily towards your preferred future. They may even become suspicious of you!(Why is she suddenly being so nice? She wants my job!)

Previously an undesired result may have made you give up. You tried something and it felt like you failed. However, in Solution Focused living, whatever happens is simply 'useful information' and indicates you have to try something different.

On the other hand, small changes can make a BIG difference and you might find that things improve almost immediately. Later on, I will tell a story of how doing something differently changed one woman's life overnight.

Noticing: as a small step

In complex situations or where you feel very disempowered and unsure of whether there is anything worth trying, a very useful and simple exercise is to actively take note of any times your preferred future is happening over the next week. This small step will help you focus on exceptions and clues to solutions.

This is a particularly good one to use if you are looking for improvement in a relationship or a behaviour change in another person. A few years ago, a friend of mine told me that he had improved his relationship with his teenage son because he noticed that the only time they had conflict-free conversations was when text messaging. So he just communicated like that with his son (even when then were in the same house!) and gradually their relationship improved. Similarly, I have worked with nursing staff in a dementia care home who used this technique very effectively to work out what strategies to use to care for their very disabled residents.

As before, make a note of what conditions are supporting these exceptions. *What are you or others doing? What is happening around you?* This is all vital information to help build solutions toward your preferred future.

Sometimes it is helpful to think about the 'signs' that your preferred future is beginning to happen. *What would those first small signs be?*

In the Solution Focused world we often wonder whether it is the 'action' or the 'visualisation of the future' that generates change. It seems that both are required.[2]Without action, intentional or not, nothing is likely to change. But taking action without clear purpose can lead you down the wrong track, wasting precious time and resources.

No matter what your situation, there is always something small you can do or change every.

---

[2]Oettingen, Schnetter and Pak showed this in their research on goal attainment in 2001

No matter

what your situation,

there is always

something small

you can do or change

every day.

Chapter Four

Solution Focused living

Solution Focus is a fantastic tool for creating change and opening up new horizons. I hope that if you have engaged in the exercises in the last chapters, you are already seeing the benefits in your own life. Sometimes change can happen fast and be quite dramatic, turning your life around. Other times, you move slowly, but surely, towards your preferred future.

This chapter focuses not so much on change, but how you can incorporate a Solution Focus into your daily life to help you to utilise it as a general tool for living. Life is complex and often complicated and there is much which is out of our direct control. Our emotions, the actions of others, the weather, and world events are all shifting and transient. We all know how easy it is to be disheartened, knocked off-course or distracted from our focus on what we want from the future.

Solution Focus can provide a stabilising force in your life, a set of tools which can always be drawn upon to help you to realign to your purpose and goals. The tools can provide a great antidote to despair, helplessness and boredom. And like all tools, the more you practice using them, the more skilled you become.

I often get people commenting on my ability to move on after adverse events. I wasn't always so resilient. For a lot of my early life I was miserable and felt sorry for myself.I felt the world was against me and lifewas a constant struggle. Living with a Solution Focus slowly shifted those feelings and as I noticed that I was able to move beyond disappointment and disasters, I began to discover my own strengths and resources more and more.

Another comment I hear is that I am very creative and visionary. I often come up with a lot of interesting ideas at work. Some of that is innate as I've always had a good imagination, but Solution Focus encourages thinking about multiple possibilities, however improbable! The aspect which is liberating is the use of small steps as experiments - I never have to invest too much before deciding if a particular course is worth pursuing.

Solution Focus has also enriched my relationships with other people, in particular my children. When you move beyond seeing people as problems, your need to criticise and correct fades away. Your ability to develop better relationship skills expands.

The best thing of all about Solution Focus is that you get to be you, not some mythical perfect person. What an amazing gift.

Keep it Simple

Steve de Shazer, one of the founders of this process said that Solution Focused approach was based on three simple statements.

1. **If it isn't broke, don't fix it.**

2. **If it's not working, do something different.**

3. **Once you know what works, do more of it.**

I find these three statement to be verypowerful if you find yourself getting sucked into being problem-focused, feeling stuck or hopeless. Each one points to part of the solution focused process and can jog your memory.

1.If it ain't broke, don't fix it!

Remember to look for exceptions rather than for something to fix when you are confronted with something that you want to change.

Exceptions are times when things are going well or indicate times when your preferred future is happening now.

When times are difficult or you are feeling bad about yourself and feel you need to change, the most useful thing you can do is stop and search for what is going well (or something you would like to continue to have in your life).

There is an English expression, "Don't throw the baby out with the bathwater." This sounds easy but when you are in the middle of a crisis it is extremely tempting to revert to problem-solving: looking for something broken, something missing or something which needs to be removed. Unless you are mending a broken bicycle or some other mechanical object, all this tends to do is to create more problems than when you started.

I used to see families as part of my work in mental health services. The kind of solution a problem-focused approach produced were things like: one member of the family was identified as disruptive, manipulative or aggressive and that person had to change. Or the family's 'communication pattern was dysfunctional' and had to be corrected.

Not surprisingly, the family or person involved felt attacked or disempowered. Instead, I would ask the family to tell me about when they *functioned well together.*"What was happening?" and "What was each of them contributing to this?"If there was one person who had been identified as a problem, I would ask the other family members what they *valued* about him or her and "What they were like when they were at their best?"

During this process many strengths, qualities and resources would become obvious. They family were not considered broken, hopeless or helpless. It is a lot easier to make hard changes if you feel you are at least a little competent and able to do the work. Once you know what is sound and working, you can build a better future on that foundation.

EXERCISE: *If your life were to change substantially, what aspects of your current life would you want to bring with you?*

2.If it's not working, do something different.

There is a famous quote attributed to Albert Einstein, "The definition of insanity is doing the same thing over and over and expecting a different outcome."Why would anyone do that? Yet that is exactly what we all do and have done at some point in our lives.

There is research on change that suggests we often think that we are doing something different but in fact it is more of the same so it doesn't make any difference!

Parenting conflicts are a common source of this kind of frustration. We want our child to do something and we try lots of different strategies, but at heart they are all forms of coercion. We feel that we have 'tried everything' and resort to louder shouting or endless grounding.

People in unsuccessful relationships often realise that although they pick different partners, over time, they all share something in common - such as being emotionally unavailable or unreliable.

The idea of doing something really different has two main benefits in Solution Focused living. First, it breaks a pattern and will inevitably produce some kind of change. Once change happens, this breaks the sense of being stuck. Secondly, it can produce change that is positive and becomes part of the information about 'what works', at least for now.

Consequently, Solution Focused living works well on a totally personal, unique level. The action which works for one person may not work for another. But somehow when people decide to do something different, they draw on their expert understanding of the situation. In Solution Focus, we say "People are experts in their own lives" - because they have been living it!

Early on in my career as a solution focused therapist a client taught me this lesson in a unique way.

Ellen was a middle-aged lady who had been diagnosed with depression. When she came to see me she told me a sad story of being taken for granted by her husband and two teenage sons. The situation at home was such that she felt that she was simply their housemaid. Her husband and children all spent time in their own rooms, only emerging for meals which she cooked. The rest of the time she was cleaning or lonely. She had tried everything to get them to change but ended up feeling alienated and powerless.

Ellen's 'preferred future' sounded quite unrealistic to me. In it, her husband would be attentive, taking her dancing once a week. Her children would be helping with the housework. They also would be spending time together as a family doing activities at the weekend. This seemed a huge shift from the pattern that had clearly built up over years. I was very new to Solution Focus and wasn't really sure what to say to her at the end of the first session. So I just suggested she *"do something different."*

I didn't see her for another five weeks as it was the Winter break. When she arrived I hardly recognised her. She looked fantastic; glowing, well-dressed and smiling. She told me that her situation had completely changed and that it was now like her preferred future. I was stunned and asked what had happened. She said, *"I did what you told me to do. I did something different."*

She told me that after our previous session she had gone home and at around 6pm when she normally started cooking, she had tried to get the sons to bring down their dirty clothes. She was ignored as usual. So she went into the living room, took out a CD of Heavy Rock, put it on extremely loud and started dancing wildly! Her family appeared and she ignored them and just continued dancing. Who knows what they must have thought? But they tidied up the house around her, made dinner and after that, everything had changed.

I have heard many similar stories, not always so dramatic but no less inspiring. I have no idea why this worked for Ellen and there is little point theorising. Somehow she knew what to do because this was her life, her husband, her children and her unique situation.

3. Once you know what works, do more of it.

Solution Focused living is about finding what works, by looking for exceptions in the present or past or by trying out different ways to move forward. When you have a clear vision for the future, it acts as compass and you can identify signs to look out for along the way.

Sometimes these exceptions and signs are obvious. Sometimes you have to work harder to identify them. However, once you know what works and do more of that, your life becomes easier and you feel more 'in the flow'.

Sometimes you will forget what works or lose trust in it. Don't beat yourself up! Occasionally what works is not something you really want to do, but it is easier to muster the motivation to do it. The more that you spend time generating a vision of the outcome you want and use it to look for exceptions or as the basis for small experimental steps to take, the more confidence you will have that Solution Focused living is a wonderful, sane, compassionate and effective way to live.

If it ain't broken
don't fix it.

If it's not working
do something different.

Once you know
what works,
do more of it.

Staying on track

Now that you have a clear idea of where you are heading, a sense of your strengths and resources and the next small step you are going to take, you might thinkthat all you now have to do is to is to sit back and enjoy the journey. Sometimes things do go smoothly and a situation resolves quickly, but more often the path is a little bumpier.

Review and Repeat

It is a good idea to set a time to review your progress. Once a week, is usually enough. The first question to ask yourself is *'what has gone well?'* Write a list of all the things which you are pleased to notice about the week just passed. Then ask yourself *'How did I do that?'* for each one on your list. This way you will start to build up knowledge about what works. If you prefer you can do this with a scale - some people find the structure of the scale helpful. You may decide to use a journal to record your answers.

Once you are satisfied that you are on track, then simply decide on your next small step.

Check in with your future perfect - is it still what you want? Maybe you need to adjust it.

I remember Louise, a middle aged woman who had developed severe anxiety at work. We had discussed how she would return to work. She had described in detail how she would walk into the workplace, greet people, do her job and she had left the session with a clear first step. A fortnight later when she came to see me she was in a quandary. *'I kept thinking about my preferred future and I've come to the conclusion that I don't really want to return to work at all. I've had enough of being the high pressure executive.* 'I asked if she would like to start over and explore a different future. She agreed and this time, having identified that she loved flower arranging, she described having her own business as a florist.

Her next small step was to discuss this with her husband. Although he was initially a little concerned that she had really gone off the rails, he came round when he realised how serious she was and together they looked at their finances and a business plan. Six months later I received a thank you note from her enclosing her business card for bespoke wedding and occasion flowers.

In the first few weeks you may achieve far more than you ever thought you could. Like Ellen in the previous section who turned her life round overnight, you might need to expand your horizons and set yourself bigger challenges. However, it is also possible that your initial assessment of your situation was over-optimistic.

Solution Focus is not a magical method to make your dreams come true. It is a way of engaging with reality, finding out what works in the situation you are in. If you ignore reality, it will remind you.

Carole came to see me about a conflict she was having with her in-laws. She wanted them to stop interfering with her life. Once she started the Solution Focused process when she returned to see me she told me that she had realised the situation was much more complex than she had first thought. Instead of feeling demoralised, she felt relieved. The reason that she was having ongoing difficulties was not her inadequacies, but the complexity of the situation. She was then able to identify her next small step in a more realistic way, focusing on something over which she had some control.

Dealing with setbacks

I used to tell my children, "there is no need to create drama in your life, life will give you all the challenges you need."We would all love to be able to control the world and those around us. None of us know what is round the corner.

We may be making excellent progress and then something happens which sets us back; a nasty remark, becoming unwell, an unexpected bill, and so on. It is easy to become disheartened or distracted at this point.

The fastest way to get back on track is to use a scale. The scale was number two of the 'preferred future' questions. If you haven't used a scale before then it might be worth rereading that section.

> **On a scale of 1 to 10, where 10 is the best you want for your life and 0 is the worst it's ever been, where are you now?**
>
> **What is going ok?**

Remind yourself of where you were heading and remember that wherever you are right now, there is always a small next step you can take. There is no need to waste time bemoaning your bad luck, venting your anger or blaming the world (unless you want to, of course!).In the end, you still have to start from where you find yourself. This attitude will gradually make you feel more resilient.

Falling off the wagon

If you are working towards a lifestyle change such as losing weight or reducing your intake of cigarettes or alcohol or increasing your exercise levels, you might find that you slip and indulge yourself. You might feel that all the hard work you've put in has all been for nothing. You feel a failure, useless, like you have no will power.

None of these thoughts are remotely useful. For one, they are unrealistic. Changing habits is incredibly hard. It is perfectly natural to slip up occasionally.

Just stop, and think, how often in the past week you were able to stay on track. Now *that* is more interesting, isn't it? I would recommend becoming very curious about how you did that. Write down every single strategy you used each time you said 'no' to something or made a positive choice. Try and recollect everything about that time. This is all proof that you CAN do it.

Remember:

Find what works and do more of it!

When I finally gave up cigarettes I found that the strategy that worked best for me was to think, 'what would a non-smoker do?' every time I had an urge to smoke.

I hit on it because I was trying to think back to something in my past which would prove I could do something I thought was impossible. I remembered that I had really struggled to learn to drive and was convinced that I would never be able to. Then I thought to myself, there are an awful lot of people who drive and I can't be that different to them. I passed my driving test a few weeks later.

So I then applied it to not smoking. I had always had excuses for why I needed a cigarette. However, there are a lot of people who manage their lives perfectly well without reaching for a cigarette. I became curious. What did they do instead?

Solution Focus is all about finding what works for you and the best place to find that is in your own life. If you can't find it then just try out different things until you hit on what works.

Confidence and Motivation

Remember I said right at the beginning of this book that Solution Focus is simple but not easy? Achieving goals, changing habits or resolving situations which have been stuck for some time generally involve a degree of hard work. The good news is that if you have done all the exercises so far, you should at least be really motivated to do all that work.

If you aren't, then maybe you haven't been entirely honest about what you want. Perhaps you have been thinking about what you *should* or *ought* to be doing rather than what really matters to you. Maybe you thought it was what you wanted but now realise that it isn't so important and that what you have right now is good enough.

You can use scales to help determine whether you are really committed to your preferred future. Here are two useful scales:

On a scale of 1 to 10, how *confident* are you that you can achieve your future perfect? Where 10 is totally confident and 0 is not at all.

Where are you now?

On a scale of 1 to 10, how *motivated* are you that you can achieve your future perfect? Where 10 is totally motivated and 0 is not at all.

Where are you now?

This can be a very revealing exercise. If you have high confidence and low motivation, then ask yourself what would need to be different for you to score somewhere between 7 and 10 for motivation. If you have high motivation but low confidence, ask yourself what you need in order to get from your low score to the next number, say 2 to 3. You might need to get help or support from others until your confidence is high enough to go it alone. Playing around with scaling in this way is very helpful to clarify exactly what you need to do and if you are likely to take the necessary step forward.

Remember that small steps are mini-experiments and do not get discouraged if they do not bring the result you anticipated. Perhaps you need to do something different. Perhaps you have learned something new about the situation which now leads you to another step. You may even end up doing something completely different.

If it's not working, do something different!

Ann was a single mother constantly in conflict with her teenage daughter. After discussing how she would prefer their relationship to be and identifying the times when this was already happening a little bit, she came up with a small step to try. When I met with her again she was eager to tell me how much better things were. I asked her what she had done. She said, '*In the end I didn't do my small step. When my daughter got home I was in a completely different space and we just sat down and chatted. We were somehow able to talk honestly about how we felt about things and got a lot sorted out.* 'This is not uncommon. Somehow just envisioning a different future, describing it and experiencing it, even virtually, creates a shift in perspective. You have moved into a Solution Focus!

Coping When Life is Hard

Sometimes life is really hard

Most people struggle at some point in their lives to a greater or lesser extent. While it is always tempting to imagine that you can ward off all danger, in reality you are not immune to the random nature of the world. You can certainly minimise risk and you can try to behave wisely but ultimately you live in a complex and uncertain world where sometimes bad things happen.

Some people think that you attract or create all that happens to you. It is true that your attitude and actions can create your reality. However, it is quite unhelpful to believe that is true for *everything* that happens to you, because when things go wrong you can only blame yourself. If a lot of things go wrong you may begin to feel you do not deserve to have good things in your life, or worse, that you are cursed, and give up trying.

On the other hand, you might think that everything that happens to you is *nothing* to do with you because it's everybody else's fault or the external world. In this case, you may find it hard to believe that it is worth taking any action because you think nothing you do makes any difference. You may think there is no point trying and even feel annoyed with friends who try to give you advice or encouragement. *"Don't they understand? I've tried everything?"* you think.

In reality we need a bit of both perspectives and this is what the famous 'Serenity Prayer' is trying to tell us:

> *Lord, grant me the serenity*
> *to accept the things I cannot change,*
> *the courage to change the things I can*
> *and the wisdom to know the difference.*

If we find ourselves stuck in a seemingly hopeless or overwhelming situation, sometimes it helps to stop and just notice how we are coping.

EXERCISE: How are you stopping things getting worse than they already are?

Are you giving yourself enough credit for how well you are actually doing?

Make a list of at least **30 things** you are doing well.

I recall working with a young woman, Emily, who came to see me because, she said, she 'wasn't coping'. I enquired about what had brought her to see me, and Emily said she felt bad because her cat had died and she couldn't stop crying. I enquired about her experience of bereavement and she told me that in the last year her father had died. Then her grandmother had died. Then an aunt had died. Now her cat had died and she'd gone to pieces. Along the way she told me about some other things that had gone wrong in her life.

I looked down at the piece of paper where I had written her answers and then asked Emily, "*What would 'coping well' look like?*"She told me that she wouldn't be crying, she'd be going to work, seeing her friends, and so on - basically describing a normal life. I turned round the piece of paper and said to her, "Could you please look at this list and tell me how you would describe a person who had experienced all this in a year and just went about their normal life?"She looked at it and answered."*Heartless, inhuman!*"

She then was then able to see her actions differently. This is called 'reframing'; when we are able to re-describe our actions to tell a more useful story. Emily could see that crying provided a release of the accumulated grief. That occasionally dampening her feelings with a glass of wine wasn't a sign of impending alcoholism, but a way to give herself a little respite. She could see that her friends were a willing support network and that she wasn't taking up all their time.

Once she'd allowed herself to be human, to have feelings, reactions and need a bit of support sometimes, she was able to think about the small steps she could take to move beyond her grief.

If we find ourselves

stuck in a

seemingly hopeless

or

overwhelming situation,

sometimes it helps

to stop and just notice

how we are coping.

Coping with a Chronic Condition

In the section about *Mining for Exceptions* I suggested that if your score on a scale was 0 or 1 you should come to this section.

I worked for a while with people living with chronic pain. They almost always scored themselves at 0 or 1 on the scale.This is lower than most of the seriously depressed people with whom I worked and tells you something about how horrible it must be to live with pain all the time.

Many people with chronic pain have ended up with lives that are extremely reduced. They rarely go out. They don't see friends and often hardly move out of a chair or bed. As you can imagine, this leads to extreme hopelessness about the future. I wondered if Solution Focus might be too much for this group of people.

I was wrong. In fact, it often seems that Solution Focus works best when things are at their worst and apparently most hopeless. Instead of asking people about their future, I decided to get them to tell me about their past, when things were going well. Without exception, people with chronic pain told me they "wanted their life back" so it seemed obvious to start there.

This might sound odd, starting with something which seems unrealistic and unattainable. But just like visualising a preferred future, this is simply a way to hook yourself into what is important and meaningful to you. Everyone is allowed to dream.

One woman, Mary, described her former social life of coffee mornings and dinner parties. Having noted that she was still extremely beautifully dressed and made up, I asked her what might be the smallest step she could take to regaining this life. She said she could phone a friend. The week after Mary invited this friend round for coffee. The following week she invited a few more friends, having decided that it was alright to use a supermarket cake instead of one she had baked herself.

Another creative lady worked out that she could go to a gallery and see the art she loved as long as she could spend the whole of the next day recovering in bed. I met her some years later by chance. She had completed an Open University degree in Art History and also introduced me to her husband whom she had met on the course!

It is people like these who have convinced me that even when things seem hopeless, it is important to focus on how you would like your life to be. Accept and honour where you are right now. Then take small steps towards your better future. This is far more useful than spending your time trying to work out how you got into your problem situation, trying to fix it or looking for a cure. In the end, the best use of your energy is to focus on the solution and move slowly towards it.

I genuinely believe this is a function of human nature. We are designed to overcome our difficulties through creativity, persistence and the stubborn pursuit of something better. Think of all the dreadful natural disasters we endure and overcome such as earthquakes, floods and hurricanes. Despite devastation and loss, time and time again, people overcome disaster, rebuild and flourish, adapting to new realities, however harsh.

Solution Focus is not new, but it is has been an unrecognised way to survive and thrive for far too long. Wherever you find yourself, in whatever dire straits, there is always something small you can do every day that can make a difference.

Never give up!

Being Solution Focused

I was sitting talking to a colleague recently and she said to me, "I really like working with you, you are always so calm, you never stop to get angry or blame others, you just get on with things."I was quite amused by this because any of my close friends (especially my office mate) will tell you that I do get angry and am very passionate in my opinions. I'm extremely idealistic; I have always wanted to help people and make the world a better place. Frequent disappointment is the flipside to idealism!

However, reflecting on what she said, it struck me that over the years I have gradually become more and more solution focused. From being a technique I once learned to help others, it has become a way of being. I rarely spend any time picking at a problem. I usually focus on the desired outcome in any situation before deciding what to do. I spend time every day noticing what is going well and what I am grateful for. I notice what other people are doing well and let them know. I listen to other people's ideas and collaborate when I can. I don't feed other people's problems by engaging in endless conversations about what's not working.

I wasn't always like this. I used to get angry and upset frequently. I felt that the world was against me, that nothing ever went right. I felt disadvantaged by having had a lonely and, at times, violent childhood. I found it hard to make friends and later, to form healthy relationships. While conventional psychotherapy had helped me understand why I felt this way it never really helped me to move beyond it.

Solution Focus provided me with a path out of my unhappiness. One small step at a time! At first it was very hard because it had been so long since I'd focused consciously on what I wanted, I didn't really know what that was. I found it almost impossible to answer any of the future focused questions. For a long time I just looked for exceptions and gradually began to become more aware of myself and my dreams and aspirations. Finally I was able to explore what I wanted.

This points to something interesting! There is a myth that to succeed the most important thing is to visualise the future. Some people say that is all you have to do. However, this has largely been disproven by research. It is important to have some kind of idea of the future you would prefer. In previous chapters, there are plenty of exercises to help you generate ideas; even something as simple as turning round a complaint by asking yourself what you would like 'instead'. That may not be a fully formed description of your ideal future, but it is enough to create a 'compass' to help you move forwards.

If visualising the future is not the key element to change, then what is? The research suggests that the most important thing is to be able to be realistic about where you are right now and then to move forwards from there.

The tricky bit is what does it mean to be 'realistic'? If you have had a lot of disappointments or if you have developed self-limiting beliefs (like: I am 'no good at' something) then you may be in the habit of seeing where you are right now as hopeless or inadequate. Using the exception questions will help you to see the good and the potential in your current situation as well as the bad and the elements you want to change. This is a more balanced and therefore, realistic, starting point. You can re-read chapters 3 and 4 for exercises to help you generate exceptions.

A really good question to ask yourself when thinking about change, is *'what do I want to keep from my life right now?'*I have made some major changes throughout my life; getting married, moving long distances, having children. Looking back, I wish I had thought a little more about what I wanted to keep. I think I lost some special people and activities, which were important to me. Being more conscious of what we have that works can lead to a feeling of greater control and appreciation of oneself.

Once you have a more realistic platform on which to move forwards and build solutions, depending on your preferred future, you may find it requires you to behave differently. This is especially true with desired changes which involve relationships with other people or taking on a new role. Sometimes this feels strange and even dishonest. One way to overcome this is to decide that you will behave 'as if' you already are that future person you wish to become. It feels like acting; at first you feel a little fake and think people will see through you. Stick with it though and soon you will grow into the new role.

Being solution focused hasn't turned me in to a different person. Instead my experience of life has changed. I find that I can bounce back from adversity quicker so I have become more resilient. In turn, this has increased my confidence in myself and my decision-making. It is as if a space has opened up where I have time to breathe and think. There is no longer a sense of panic and dread.

Having discovered my 'best self' through exploring exceptions, I can call on it when needed. I am braver than previously and more willing to take on a challenge, more willing to say, "Yes". For example, in 2014 I agreed to give a TEDx talk. Initially I felt very nervous, and began to wonder if I had overstretched myself.

Having prepared as well as possible I thought about what I wanted from the experience. I realised that most of all I wanted to enjoy myself. Although I wanted to do my best, I didn't want to spend the day worrying about my slot, and afterwards, I didn't want to spend time criticising myself and wishing I had done it differently. So I thought about how I would be at my best when enjoying the experience.

On the day I was relaxed and enjoyed all the other speakers. When it was my turn, I felt excited and a little nervous. I had to do the talk without notes and my memory let me down a couple of times, but overall I was happy because I had achieved what I wanted.

It is tempting to say that this success occurred because I had lowered my expectations. I disagree. If I had wanted something different from the experience, let's say I wanted to deliver a perfect talk; I would have done different things to prepare for the event. I would not have minded the nerves. I would not have been interested in the other speakers, but spent my time rehearsing to ensure my talk went perfectly. I would have done what it would take. However, that is not the outcome I wanted.

In the past I might well have felt I *ought* to try to do a perfect talk. But it would have been just that; an obligation I felt towards others. Then, I would have worried about 'getting it right'. I spent a lot of my life worrying about what other people thought of me. It was quite exhausting! Having said that, my goal of enjoying myself was not an easy option. I have high standards and I wanted to do well and having enjoyment as a goal was a big risk. It was a new experience from which I learned a great deal.

The Power of Small Steps

In Chapter 4 I talked about small steps as little 'experiments' and how this is different to goal-setting. When we set goals, they are a kind of responsibility, a commitment to achieve no matter what. Or they are imagined landmarks on the way to achieving success or change. We set them in the belief that they are possible and also that they will be effective in moving us towards our ultimate aims. While this is often true, it is also the case that goals can be limiting and unrealistic.

They are limiting because we exclude other possibilities. They do not allow for new or serendipitous solutions and it is hard to deviate from a goal path even if it is not working. Instead, we tend to become even more focused - a bit like the fabled Englishman who simply speaks louder in order to make himself understood to a foreigner! We are also limited to what we know already. If we are problem-focused, then goals are often related to a solution to a specific problem, so the goal is limited by problem thinking.

I also describe goals as unrealistic because they require us to believe that we can foretell how the future will unfold. We have no idea what is going to happen tomorrow! Have any of you ever had an imaginary conversation with someone in your head and then found that it went very differently in real life? All of life is like that. Our imagination is a powerful tool for generating the future, but not for controlling it. HOW things happen is different to the way we imagine it, most of the time. When things go to plan, we are generally surprised.

So I have found changing my mindset from goals to small steps to be one of the greatest tools and benefits of Solution Focused living. I chose to call this book 'The Power of the Next Small Step' because I think this is the key to successful living. Once you really GET that small steps are experiments towards the future you want, life becomes much less stressful.

You don't have to try to control the future (an impossible task!) and you do not waste energy trying to work out what went wrong when things inevitably do. Most important of all, you gradually stop blaming yourself and others for what does or does not happen. You stop trying to be a fortune-telling automaton. You get to be human.

Try something out, if it works and is bringing you closer to what you want, then do more of it or build on it. If it doesn't work, then *do something different* and see what happens. You are using the same kind of thinking skills as goal-setting but with a completely different attitude. I think of this like the difference between having a 'know-it-all' attitude and an open, learning attitude. I am willing for the universe to teach me about myself and what works. It is a way of co-operating with life instead of grappling with it and trying to bend it to your will. It's the difference between the mindset of 'I wonder if...?' and 'I know that...'

The next small step gets its power from the work you have done creating an imagined preferred future. In Chapter 2 I went through different exercises you can do in order to generate a clear picture of the way you would like your life to be. Once you have a sense of what this will be like, then you know where to put your efforts. By taking small steps every day the path to your preferred future rolls out before you. You do not have to create the path first. This is the biggest mistake people make. They want to map out the path and *then* take steps, checking along the way if they are 'on track'.

It seems logical, but life tends to be a much messier affair. With small steps you can start wherever you are; being blown off-course or being distracted or even suffering a severe setback are not the disasters they would be if you felt obliged to stay on a particular path. As long as you know where you're headed, you can take a step in that direction from wherever you find yourself.

The preferred future is often, at heart, an abstract concept such as 'feeling at peace with myself' or 'being able to support my children'. In Solution Focus you are encouraged to describe in detail what it would look like. In part this is so that when parts of your future start happening, you notice them! The other benefit is that it gives you ideas for what you can do right now - for the next small step. If having a regular meditation slot every day is part of your preferred future, then a small step could be to meditate for 5 minutes at the beginning of every weekday.

When you begin to be Solution Focused in an everyday way, you become more fearless. Trying something out is not so much of a risk because you are used to the experimental small steps you have been taking. There is no such thing as 'failure'. Instead there is merely the question of whether it worked or not - was it useful, worth repeating, educational? One of the greatest benefits I have found is that I have gradually become much gentler with myself, kinder and more compassionate. Bit by bit, the harsh demands and punishing thoughts, which I had internalised from childhood, fell away.

Finally, make sure you read Section 8, Staying on Track, so that you remain Solution Focused, rather than solution forced. It is hard to get out of the problem-solving and goal-oriented mindset. It takes a little time to understand that this is about you setting your own pace, rather than treating yourself as an under-performing employee! You will gradually find yourself collaborating with the flow of life rather than battling against it.

Remember, you are allowed to change your mind. You can create a whole different future any time you want. You can simplify the method down to:

- What do you want out of next week, out of today at work, out of this meeting?

- What is going right at the moment, what are my strengths, where are the building blocks?
- What is my next small step, or what would be the first signthat things are moving in the right direction?

The exercises in this book can be done again and again. You can adapt them to make them more meaningful to you. When you become more familiar with them, you can use the questions to move conversations with others away from problem talk.

The more you practice being Solution Focused, the easier life becomes. When setbacks occur or even disasters, you will find, once the initial upset dies away, you have the tools to pick yourself up and make a realistic assessment of where you are right now (the good as well as the bad).You can find the tiniest toehold on which you can build towards the future.

That is the power of the next small step.

Gratitude

This book did not come out of nowhere. It is built on the work of many other people and it has come to fruition because of the support of others. I would like to express my gratitude to them. It's a long list, feel free to skip it, it is an indulgence!

First of all I would like to thank Lesley Worsham for her hard work in typesetting and producing the book for publication and Brian Davis for the initial edit.

Secondly to the people who 'test drove' the book for me and gave me helpful feedback: Nicola Biggs, Julie Hilliard and Arike.

To Steve de Shazer and Insoo Kim Berg who developed solution focused brief therapy with their colleagues, first at the Mental Research Institute in Palo Alto, and then at the Brief Therapy Centre in Milwaukee.

To Evan George at BRIEF who trained me in solution focused brief therapy. Without his patience and gentle support I would not have overcome my barriers to becoming a non-expert.

To BRIEF: Chris Iveson, Harvey Ratner and Evan George, who have always supported and encouraged me and even let me run a training event for them!

To Harry Korman who manages the SFT-L online discussion list. Without the list I would not have learned so much or met solution focused practitioners throughout the world.

To Brian Cade who tolerated my playful insults and always made me feel beautiful and intelligent.

To Mark McKergow and Paul Z Jackson, who took me under their wing at the first EBTA conference and introduced me to solution focus in organisations.

To Elliott Connie for his friendship and unending support, particularly in bringing this book into being, and for being one of the most inspiring people I've ever met.

To Guy Shennan and Paul Hackett and other rogues for fantastic late night conference shennanigans.

To my friends in the United Kingdom Association of Solution Focused Practice who have worked tirelessly to promote and support the development of solution focus in the UK.

To my friends in the European Brief Therapy Association whose annual conferences provided me with space to think, be challenged and present my thoughts for debate.

For inspiring conversations online and off, with Michael Klingenstierna Hjerth, Jenny Clarke, Stephen Langer, Kirsten Dierolf, John Wheeler, Paul Hanton, Michael Durrant, Dvorah Simon, Martin Fletcher, Janine Waldman and many more.

Find a coach or therapist

If, after reading this book, you think you would prefer to work with a qualified solution focused coach or therapist, you can find one via the following organisations:

UK

United Kingdom Associate of Solution Focused Practitioners

http://www.ukasfp.co.uk

BRIEF

https://www.brief.org.uk

Europe

European Brief Therapy Association

http://ebta.eu/

<u>USA</u>

Association for Solution Focused Practitioners

http://associationforsolutionfocusedpractitioners.com/

<u>Australia</u>

Australasian Association for Solution-Focused Brief Therapy

http://www.solutionfocused.org.au/

31511688R00074

Printed in Great Britain
by Amazon